Little KID, BIG City!

LonDON

WRITTEN by
BETH BECKMAN

ILLUSTRATIONS by
HOLLEY MAHER

QUIRK BOOKS
PHILADELPHIA

FOR MY LITTLE TRAVEL BUDDY AND EXPLORER—
CAN'T WAIT TO EXPLORE MORE CITIES TOGETHER!

Library of Congress Cataloging in Publication Data
Beckman, Beth, author. | Maher, Holley, illustrator.
Little kid, big city! London / written by Beth Beckman ; illustrations by Holley Maher.
Summary: "An illustrated, chooseable-path travel guide to London"—Provided by publisher.
LCSH: London (England)—Guidebooks. | Children—Travel—England—London—Guidebooks.
LCC DA679 .B324 2021 | DDC 914.2104/86—dc23
2020054379

ISBN: 978-1-68369-248-5

Printed in China

Typeset in Argone and Wink Wink

Designed by Andie Reid
Production management by John J. McGurk

Quirk Books
215 Church Street
Philadelphia, PA 19106
quirkbooks.com

10 9 8 7 6 5 4 3 2 1

A NOTE BEFORE YOU START YOUR BIG CITY ADVENTURE

With this book, you can explore the sights, tastes, and landmarks of London! When you're ready to head to your next destination, look for the options asking where to go next and then turn to the page you chose to visit.

If you want to learn more about a place, turn to the **Adventure Index** in the back of this book for tips and fun facts.

Don't forget the **map**; it's located in the back! You can even tear it out and use it on the go.

Are you ready to explore London?
Let's get started!

LONDON IS CALLING!

Will you answer?

In this historic English city, there's plenty to do and plenty to see . . .

Got your map?

Get ready, get set . . .

LET'S GO!

Alarms sound—
here comes a tall ship!
All eyes are on the
TOWER BRIDGE!

Tower Bridge has a drawbridge that opens and closes to let ships pass underneath.

Completed in 1894, Tower Bridge was an engineering wonder. It took eight years and the daily labor of over **400 construction workers** to build. Today, visitors can climb the tall gothic towers, tour the engineering room and museum exhibitions, and brave the glass floor walkways that run high over the roaring traffic and River Thames below.

WHERE TO NEXT?

Learn about London's ravens! Turn to page **4**.
Tour a fresh food market! Turn to page **6**.

Storm the battlements and marvel at priceless treasures at this historic castle and tower!

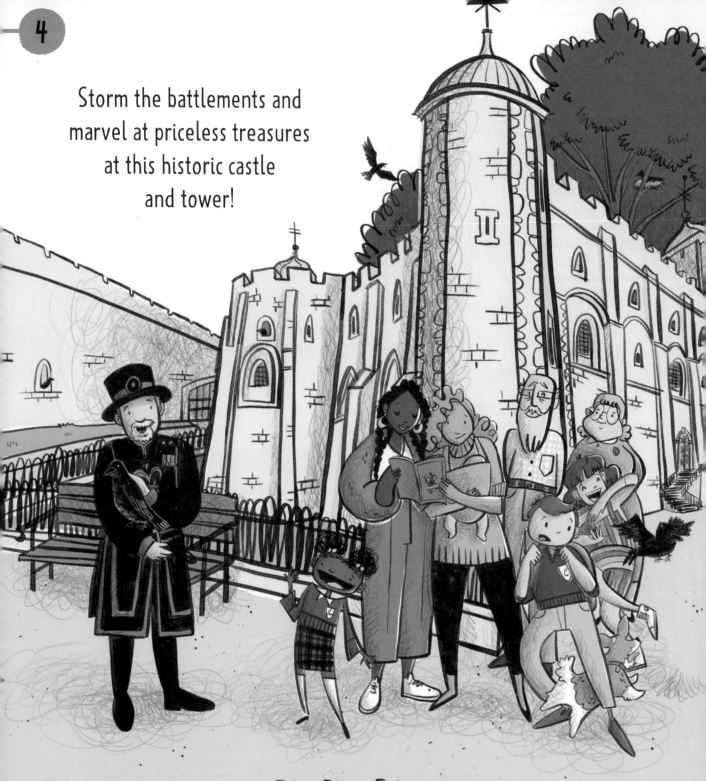

Throughout its 1,000-year history, the **TOWER OF LONDON** has been an armory, a dungeon, a mint where coins were made, a fortress, and even a zoo! Today it's the home of the ceremonial guardians of the tower, known as Beefeaters. Don't miss the iconic Beefeater tour, where you can hear gruesome tales of the tower, tour the armory's swords, and visit the famous ravens that live within the fortress walls.

Legend says that the kingdom and the Tower of London will fall if the resident ravens ever leave; in fact, **six ravens** are kept in the fortress at all times by royal decree. Are all six ravens there today?

This tightly guarded fortress has much to be seen,
from the Royal Family's jewels to crowns for kings and queens!

Prepare to be dazzled by coronation crowns, jeweled scepters, and ceremonial swords!
The twinkling artifacts contain over **23,000 REAL gemstones**. It's said to be
the most valuable jewel collection in the world!

WHERE TO NEXT?

Fill your belly with yummy foods! Turn to page **6**.
Climb to the top of a famous dome! Turn to page **8**.

Feeling peckish?
(That's British slang
for "hungry"!)
Let's grab some food at
BOROUGH MARKET!

Browse food stalls heaped with produce and feast on dishes from across the globe. Over **100 vendors** and restaurants line the market's halls. You'd better come hungry . . . there's plenty to discover (and devour) here!

WHERE TO NEXT?

Be part of a historic audience! Turn to page 10.
Learn about modern masterpieces! Turn to page 12.

Walking shoes are essential on the climb
to the top of this enormous cathedral!

Crowning **ST. PAUL'S CATHEDRAL** and weighing in at a whopping **65,000 tons**, the dome of this church is one of the city's most impressive landmarks. If you climb **528 steps** to the very top, you'll reach the Golden Gallery, which runs around the highest point of the outer dome. This gallery offers spectacular panoramic views across London!

Have a secret? In the Whispering Gallery, you can share the quietest whisper with a friend from across the room. Due to a quirk in the construction of the cathedral, sound carries perfectly along the walls of the dome.

WHERE TO NEXT?

Do you hear a phone ringing?
Turn to page **14**.

Hungry? Head over to your favorite chippie!
Turn to page **16**.

All the world's a stage at this theater dedicated
to Shakespeare and his plays!

THE GLOBE THEATRE is an open-air re-creation of the theater where
William Shakespeare's plays were performed. The original Globe Theatre
was built in 1599, but it burned down in 1613.

The replica that stands today is entirely authentic! The theater is made of wood and even has a thatched roof. Performances are still held here—and true to historical tradition, they are acted without microphones or speakers, and music is played on period instruments.

WHERE TO NEXT?

Visit the city's largest dome! Turn to page 8.
See the Queen's collection of crowns! Turn to page 4.

Explore, appreciate, play, and learn—
Do it all in the massive art gallery,
the TATE MODERN!

From Picasso to Rothko, Dalí to Matisse, the Tate Modern holds an impressive collection of modern and contemporary art from 1900 to the present day. Housed in a ginormous building that used to be a power station, the ever-rotating collections are showcased over six floors. Bold, colorful, and often quirky, there's something for everyone at the Tate!

There's no need to whisper in this museum—making noise at the Tate is encouraged! The Tate Modern loves art adventurers and even gives families suggested games to play while touring the collections. Can you strike a pose like that portrait?

WHERE TO NEXT?

Glide by London's famous buildings! Turn to page 18.
Get a bird's-eye view of the city! Turn to page 20.

I hear ringing!
Is that London calling?

This iconic red structure is a
TELEPHONE BOX
from back when the city had
public payphones! They first
appeared in 1926 and have
since become a London icon.
Today the booths serve as
decoration and nostalgic
reminders of a time before
cellphone technology.

A **PILLAR BOX** is a
free-standing post box for
mailing letters. Today these
letters are collected by mail
trucks and distributed, but in
the past they used to go on a
little adventure . . .

Something fun runs deep below London—a mysterious miniature subway system that was mostly unknown to the public!

The Mail Rail was a hidden subway system that whizzed **millions of letters and packages** underground throughout London for over 75 years. The railway is no longer in use; however, the **POSTAL MUSEUM** allows guests to climb on board these replica rail cars and ride deep in the unique underground tunnels of the subterranean railway.

WHERE TO NEXT?

Go for a wild slide ride! Turn to page **26**.
This library has literary treasures inside! Turn to page **28**.

A plate piled high with crispy battered fish, served with perfectly fried potatoes and mayonnaise for dip!

And don't forget a dash of salt and vinegar!

FISH-AND-CHIPS is one of London's signature dishes. The first fish-and-chips shop opened in East London in 1860, and today there are over **10,000 Fish and Chip shops**—known as chippies—in the United Kingdom! Chippies outnumber all other restaurants, including fast-food chains. Whether at a pub or a to-go counter, you can find fish-and-chips on almost every street corner throughout London.

WHERE TO NEXT?

Visit one of the busiest meeting spots in the city!
Turn to page 22.
Sort through London's communication history!
Turn to page 14.

Need a rest for your tired feet?
A CRUISE ON THE RIVER THAMES can't be beat!

The tumbling Thames runs through the center of London, making these boat rides perfect for sightseeing! Jump on board, grab a window seat, and relax as the cruise winds through the city.

Many of London's skyscrapers have silly nicknames based on what they look like: the **Walkie-Talkie**, the **Cheese Grater**, and the **Gerkin** are just a few. By looking at the skyline, can you see these shapes, too?

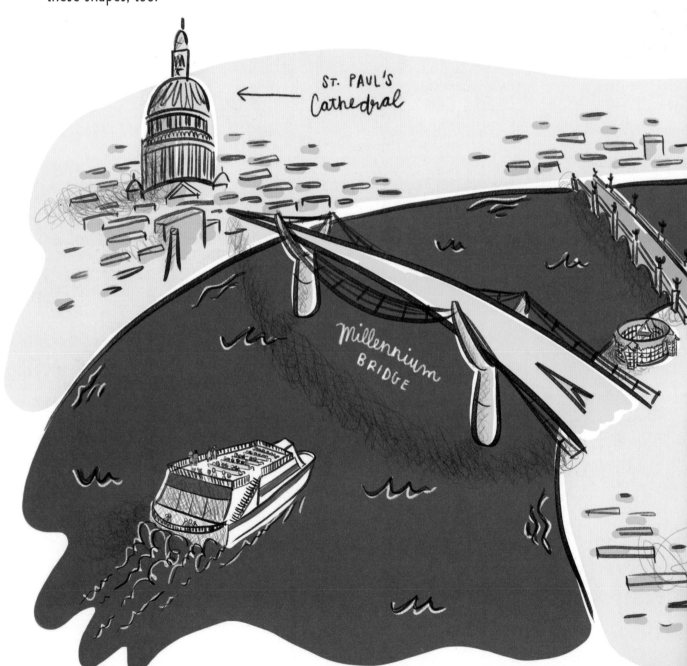

← ST. PAUL'S Cathedral

Millennium BRIDGE

The "WALKIE-TALKIE"

The "CHEESE GRATER"

The "GHERKIN"

London BRIDGE

Tower BRIDGE

WHERE TO NEXT?

Grab lunch at a local pub! Turn to page **16**.
See London from high above! Turn to page **20**.

Discover London from high in the sky
by taking a spin on the **LONDON EYE!**

Resembling a giant bicycle wheel, the London Eye is one of the tallest observation wheels in the world! Visitors ride in one of **32 state-of-the-art capsules**, which can carry up to **25 people** at a time. Towering over the River Thames at a height of **443 feet**, the London Eye gives a bird's-eye view of Big Ben, the Houses of Parliament, and most of the landmarks in London!

WHERE TO NEXT?

Cruise down the River Thames! Turn to page **18**.
See where all royal ceremonies take place! Turn to page **24**.

As the bustling center point of the city,
TRAFALGAR SQUARE
is the place to be!

The Pride of Trafalgar Square is the **four huge lion statues**. They proudly protect a tall column that holds a tiny statue of a naval hero on top.

Can you spot the empty column base? It was supposed to support a statue, but it was never made. Today, the pedestal is considered a very prestigious art space in London that offers a rotating display of artwork and installations. You never know what will be on display!

Which way next? I'm turned around . . . should we head north or west?

Why don't we ask the lions? They know best!

WHERE TO NEXT?

Head north—in this direction! Turn to page **32**.

Walk south—past the intersection! Turn to page **24**.

Or should we just follow the gaze of the lions?

Turn to page **30**.

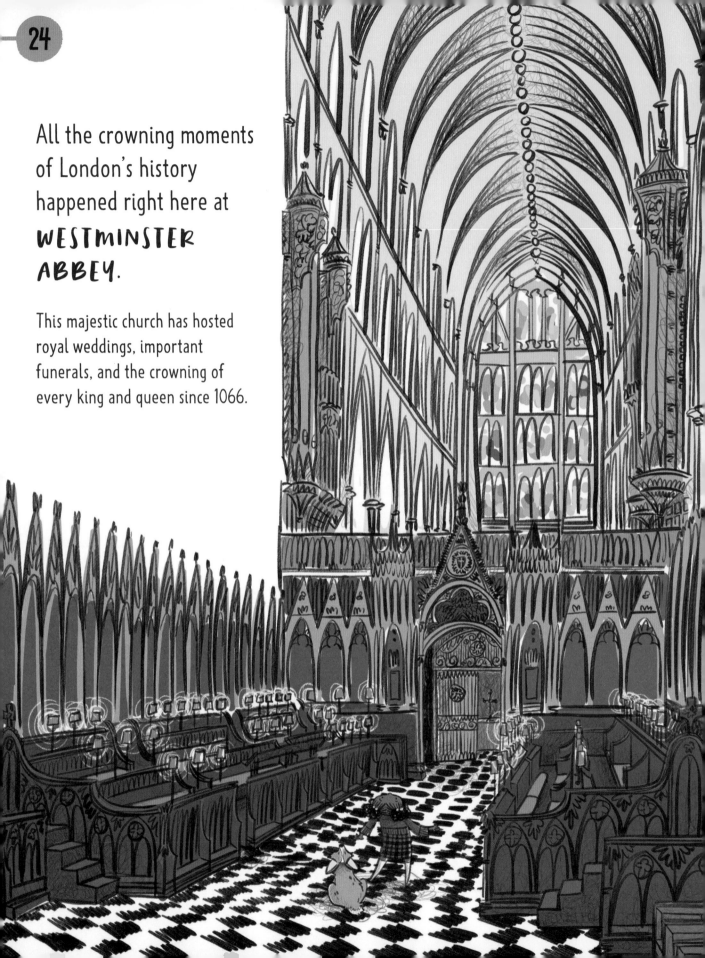

All the crowning moments of London's history happened right here at **WESTMINSTER ABBEY.**

This majestic church has hosted royal weddings, important funerals, and the crowning of every king and queen since 1066.

Inside the church you will find the **Poets' Corner**, which houses a memorial to famous poets and writers such as Charles Dickens, Oscar Wilde, and William Shakespeare, along with Jane Austen, the Brontë sisters, and many others. The Abbey is also home to the **Coronation Chair**, which is the oldest piece of furniture in all of England.

Continue your royal adventure!

WHERE TO NEXT?

Visit the home of the Queen!
Turn to page **38**.

Get lost in a royal maze! Turn to page **40**.

It's time to visit the Royal Museum!
Turn to page **42**.

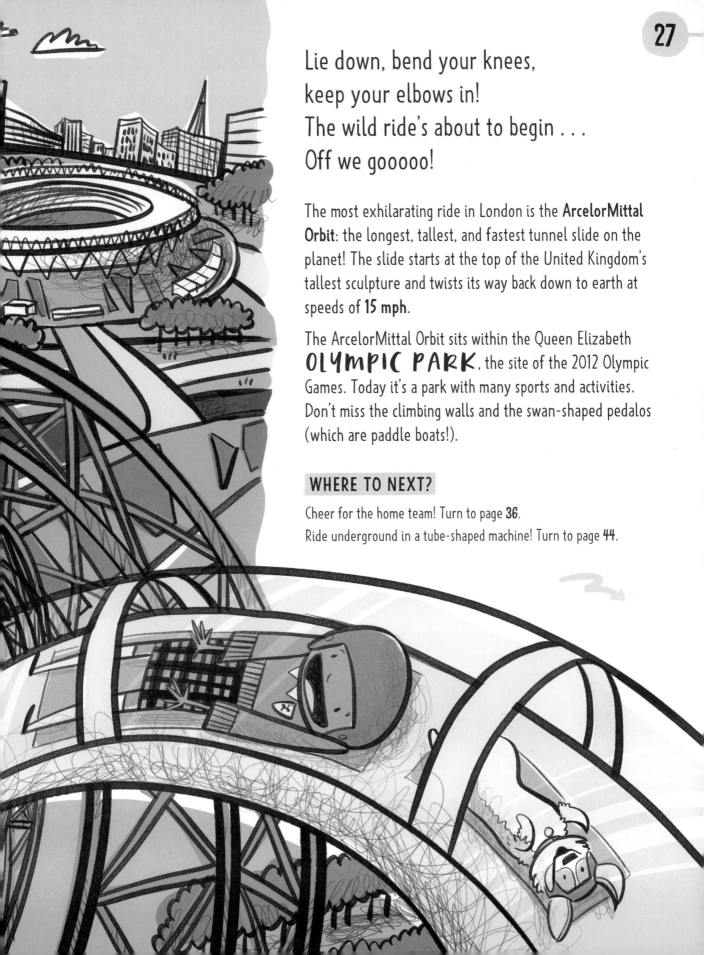

Lie down, bend your knees,
keep your elbows in!
The wild ride's about to begin . . .
Off we gooooo!

The most exhilarating ride in London is the **ArcelorMittal Orbit**: the longest, tallest, and fastest tunnel slide on the planet! The slide starts at the top of the United Kingdom's tallest sculpture and twists its way back down to earth at speeds of **15 mph**.

The ArcelorMittal Orbit sits within the Queen Elizabeth **OLYMPIC PARK**, the site of the 2012 Olympic Games. Today it's a park with many sports and activities. Don't miss the climbing walls and the swan-shaped pedalos (which are paddle boats!).

WHERE TO NEXT?

Cheer for the home team! Turn to page **36**.
Ride underground in a tube-shaped machine! Turn to page **44**.

A journey through literary history
can be found at this massive library!

The **BRITISH LIBRARY** is one of the largest libraries
on the planet! Its collections include more than **170 million items**,
and counting. Books, magazines, manuscripts, maps, musical scores,
newspapers, patents, databases, drawings, and sound recordings can
be found here in over **400 languages**. Highlights include
Leonardo da Vinci's notebook, the Beatles' original lyrics,
and the original *Alice in Wonderland* manuscript!

Where does the library keep all of these millions of treasures?

It has specialized storage areas that go WAY below the surface!

The basement of the British Library descends **80 feet below ground**—the equivalent of an eight-story building! The collections are all carefully arranged and coded, kept in strict climate-controlled conditions, and organized in state-of-the-art bookcases and shelves.

WHERE TO NEXT?

A book comes to life at this famous platform! Turn to page **52**.
Explore London's many modes of transportation! Turn to page **30**.

Climb up and into the driver's seat of this museum's historic fleet!

Iconic red buses, taxis, trains, and vintage carriages: vehicles are at the heart of the **LONDON TRANSPORT MUSEUM**, which brings to life the city's history of transportation. Jump on old buses and trains to learn how London has changed over **200 years**. Don't buses look so different today?

Get behind the steering wheel of the vintage fleet, take over the controls of the Tube in a driving simulator, and see London's first bus (powered by a horse!). It's fun to look at the past, present, and future of London's iconic transportation system.

Next, board London's current buses and trains!

WHERE TO NEXT?

Hop on and off the bus! Turn to page **53**. Visit London's busiest Tube station! Turn to page **52**.

Red paper lanterns sway in the breeze—this way to Chinatown's restaurants, shops, and bakeries!

CHINATOWN is London's Chinese community hub, and it's where visitors come to celebrate Chinese culture.

Be sure to look up! Four ornate gates mark the entrances to Chinatown. The largest gate (covered in real gold leaf) was created in Beijing and showcases ornamental designs of the Qing dynasty: glazed yellow tiles, a golden dragon, and beautifully painted panels.

Come hungry! From fresh hand-pulled noodles to savory dim sum, this neighborhood is full of delicious restaurants to tempt your tastebuds.

WHERE TO NEXT?

Showtime! Do you have your tickets?
Turn to page **58**.
Visit the best toy store on the planet!
Turn to page **60**.

Wait, a circus?
But I don't see any tents!
No trapeze acts, no clowns—
it doesn't make sense!

Circus is a Latin word meaning
"circle" or "ring," and
PICCADILLY CIRCUS is
the largest street circle in the city!

Considered the heart of the city,
Piccadilly is a popular gathering
place for tourists and locals alike.
The square is famous for its brightly
illuminated billboards, the Eros
fountain, and the wide variety of
shopping, theater, and music options
all within walking distance.

It's said that if you stand in
Piccadilly long enough, everyone
in the world will pass by. The square
is always bustling and busy. How
many people can you count?

WHERE TO NEXT?

Circle the city in a bus! Turn to page **62**.

Find a new toy to bring home with us!
Turn to page **60**.

Will that goalie stop the kick?
Our team needs to score another point, quick!

There's nothing more exciting than catching a live **FOOTBALL MATCH** in London!

Football (or soccer, as it's called in the United States) was first played in England way back in the early 1800s. Today, it is the most popular sport in not only London but the world! It's played by **250 million players** in over **200 countries**.

Drive down the gate, pass the ball!
A header and a kick, will they get it in the goal?

The crowd is on its feet!
The stands thunder with cheers . . .
They shoot . . .

GOOOAAAL!

WHERE TO NEXT?

Head back into the city to celebrate! Turn to page 44.

There's one noble residence that can't be missed— the home of royalty, BUCKINGHAM PALACE!

Valued at **1.5 billion dollars**, Buckingham Palace is one of the most expensive homes on the planet! With **775 rooms**, including **52 bedrooms** and **78 bathrooms**, it's easy to get lost in this enormous mansion. The Royal Standard Flag is flown at full mast when the Queen is in the palace. Is she home today?

Behind these ornate iron gates, a royal ceremony takes place!

The **CHANGING OF THE GUARD** is a formal ceremony performed by the soldiers guarding the palace, in which they hand over their responsibilities to a new group of soldiers. Visitors can expect a spectacular show with guardsmen on horseback, marching bands, and lots of pomp and circumstance!

WHERE TO NEXT?

Make a stop for a proper tea!
Turn to page **46**.

Take in some history!
Turn to page **48**.

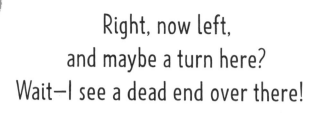

Right, now left,
and maybe a turn here?
Wait—I see a dead end over there!

Get lost at **HAMPTON COURT PALACE**, home of the United Kingdom's oldest surviving hedge maze! With over half a mile of twisting green paths, the mystifying maze takes up over a third of an acre and has been baffling visitors since the 1600s.

The maze is just one of the regal attractions at this royal palace. The **Magic Garden** is also a fun stop for families, with tall slides, fountains, and dragons, all inspired by the palace's myths and legends. Be sure to climb the colorful **King's and Queen's towers**, which offer a royal view over the area.

WHERE TO NEXT?

Say hi to London's lions! Turn to page **22**.
Salute the famous palace guardians! Turn to page **38**.

East meets West at the ROYAL OBSERVATORY,
a London museum with an important history!

The Royal Observatory is built on the **Prime Meridian**: the line running along 0° of longitude, the place where the earth's Western and Eastern Hemispheres meet. Visitors can stand astride the meridian line, technically having one foot in the Western Hemisphere and one in the Eastern Hemisphere at the same time! What side do you live on?

The Prime Meridian was a very important reference! Established in 1851, it was from this point that scientists first mapped the stars to help mariners determine their location as they sailed across the oceans.

Today you can visit the museum and discover how time, astronomy, and global exploration work together. Set your watch to the first public clock, see the iconic **Time Ball** drop, and tour London's only planetarium!

WHERE TO NEXT?

Roar on over to visit T-Rex! Turn to page **48**.

See an ancient celebration of the solstice! Turn to page **50**.

Royal
Observatory
Greenwich

Climb aboard and
mind the gap . . .
THE UNDERGROUND
gets you there in a snap!

The oldest railway in the world
is also the fastest way to get
around London!

Opened in 1863, it was once
pulled by steam engines. Today,
the Underground is a network of
trains that covers over **250 miles**
underground and above water
and carries more than 1 billion
passengers a year.

The Underground is nicknamed
the Tube because of the distinctive
shape of its arched circular tunnels
and stations.

The Tube travels FAST! Be
prepared for **60 m.p.h. speeds**
through these tube-shaped paths!

WHERE TO NEXT?

Next stop—the circus! Turn to Page **34**.
Next stop—a royal palace! Turn to Page **38**.

Tasty tiny sandwiches and delicious scones with cream . . .
There's nothing quite like a proper afternoon tea!

AFTERNOON TEA is a British tradition that was started in the 1800s by the Duchess of Bedford. The Duchess was often hungry between lunch and dinner, so she started having a hot pot of tea and snacks with friends around 3 to 5 p.m. The idea quickly spread, and teatime soon became a beloved tradition across Britain!

Afternoon tea typically consists of delicate finger sandwiches—like ham and cheese, cucumber, and egg mayonnaise—plus a selection of sweet fruit scones, butter tarts, and pastries with jam and clotted cream. And of course, don't forget the perfectly steeped tea!

WHERE TO NEXT?

Catch a world-famous stage performance!
Turn to page **58**.

Tour delightful flowering gardens!
Turn to page **56**.

No bones about it—the discoveries at the NATURAL HISTORY MUSEUM are endless!

From a moon rock as old as the solar system to one of the world's most impressive dinosaur fossil exhibitions, the Natural History Museum holds many unique treasures.

Take an escalator through planet earth, roar next to a robotic T-Rex, and see over **29 million animal specimens** in the museum's zoology collections!

The museum is home to more than **80 million items** and adds over 500,000 more each year, making it one of the largest collections of natural history in the world. What will you discover here?

WHERE TO NEXT?

Tour an ancient mystery! Turn to page **50**.

Visit the greatest park in the city! Turn to page **56**.

Magical and mysterious,
Stonehenge is a can't-miss
site for the curious!

STONEHENGE is an ancient circle
(or "henge") of huge stone slabs!

The enormous stones date back to around
2500 BCE, but how and why this monument was
built is still a mystery. Some researchers believe it
was a gathering site for feasts and celebrations that
likely revolved around the changing seasons—the
circular arrangement lines up precisely with the
sunrise and sunset on each solstice.

These large stones weigh about four tons each.
How do you think they all got here?

CONTINUE THE ADVENTURE!

Let's head back to London! Turn to page **44**.

Our train is about to depart . . . All aboard to Hogwarts!

While passing through **KING'S CROSS STATION**, Harry Potter fans should stop by Platform 9¾ on the west side of the building. Here you will find a magical trolley disappearing into the bricks . . . Is it real or just a trick?

Fans will remember that Harry Potter and his friends found the Hogwarts Express by entering a magical portal on the train platform.

No secret spell needed for us Muggles! Visitors can step right up to the trolley sculpture for a picture or visit the gift shop to pick up a magical souvenir.

WHERE TO NEXT?

Explore a wild kingdom!
Turn to page **54**.

Kick it over to the stadium!
Turn to page **36**.

Here comes the bus, hop on board—
swipe your card in the reader, we're ready to explore!

Grab a window seat. Look over there, I see Hamleys!
There's Westminster Abbey! Ready to jump off?
Just push the button! At the next stop you can
exit and continue your city exploration!

Wheeling through London is
so much fun while riding on
a double-decker bus.

WHERE TO NEXT?

Hop off to some of the city's best graffiti! Turn to page **64**.
Hop off at a yummy bakery! Turn to page **32**.

A wild world of animals awaits behind these historic Regent Park gates!

Opened to the public in 1847, the **ZSL LONDON ZOO** was the first to open a zoo area designed specifically for children. It was also home to the world's first public aquarium.

Lions, tigers, and penguins—oh my! Today the zoo sits on **36 acres** and is home to over **750 species**, making it the largest animal collection in the United Kingdom. Find your pride in the Land of the Lions exhibit, get your stripes in the Tiger Territory, and waddle around Penguin Beach to watch a feeding—there's so much to do at the zoo!

WHERE TO NEXT?

Visit a colorful neighborhood! Turn to page **68**.
Ride on a narrowboat! Turn to page **66**.

A lush oasis and garden—
it's easy to forget you're
in the heart of London!

HYDE PARK is one of the largest parks
in London. Sail across the Serpentine River,
saddle up for a ride on horseback, and check out
the Princess Diana memorial playground based
on Peter Pan!

Have a message to share? Speech is free at
the **Speaker's Corner**, where anyone is invited
to jump on a podium to voice their opinions.

No arguments here: Hyde Park has something
for everyone!

WHERE TO NEXT?

Have a wild animal encounter! Turn to page **54**.
See a charming neighborhood from
the water! Turn to page **66**.

The curtain rises
and the lights dim . . .
The stage show is
about to begin!

With over 200 theater spaces
around town, London is considered
the theater capital of the world.
THE WEST END (also
known as Theatreland) is the
celebrated center of London's
performing arts scene, with over
40 grand playhouses and large-
scale performance stages in the
area. From modern-day adaptations
to family-friendly musicals like
Matilda and *Mary Poppins*, there's
always an element of fun
to be found on London's
enchanting stages.

WHERE TO NEXT?

The curtain is closing on our day.
Grab a cab for one last adventure!
Turn to page **70**.

A world of wonder awaits at this toy shop dedicated to fun and play!

In search of a special doll, the perfect book, or the best building set? **HAMLEYS** iconic flagship store has seven floors stuffed full of games, crafts, and nearly any toy you can imagine!

This delightful shop is known for having the cuddliest stuffed toys in the world—it sells a teddy bear every two minutes! Since its opening in 1760, Hamleys has sold over **15 million bears**!

Toys here don't just stay on the shelves—they come to life! Hamley and Hattie Bear are frequent guests at store events, and the playful staff entertains visitors with activities and live toy demonstrations. Every day is a celebration at Hamleys!

WHERE TO NEXT?

Sip some yummy tea! Turn to page **46**.

Grab your tickets—there's a show to see!
Turn to page **58**.

SWEET SHOP

Ready to hop on board?
The **DOUBLE-DECKER BUS** is a fun way to explore!

London's iconic red buses are a convenient, inexpensive way to get around the city. Climb on—watch your step!—and head to the upper deck. The view here is the best way to see the sights.

Wondering why the buses are red? Before 1907, buses were painted different colors to match their route. There was fierce competition between the bus companies, and one of them painted its fleet red to stand out from the crowd. A century later, most companies have chosen to paint their buses the same cherry-red color.

WHERE TO NEXT?

Voice your opinion at this famous corner! Turn to page **56**.
A magical world of toys to discover! Turn to page **60**.

Swing by Brick Lane and stay a while to explore street art, shopping, and Curry Mile!

Rich with history and home to one of the largest Bangladeshi communities outside of South Asia, **BRICK LANE** is best known for its diverse artistic and cultural activities and bustling atmosphere. Check out the world-renowned street art, galleries, vintage record shops, and one-of-a-kind clothing stalls.

If it's curry you're craving, you've come to the right place! Brick Lane is known as London's **Curry Mile**, thanks to the many restaurants that line the street. Savory chicken and rice, coconut chutney, and sweet baklava . . . What'll you have to eat?

WHERE TO NEXT?

Cast a spell at this magical platform! Turn to page **52**.

Say hello to this square's stone guardians! Turn to page **22**.

No need to travel by foot—Canals are the best way to explore this unique neighborhood!

LITTLE VENICE is
known for making a splash!

Just like the famous city in Italy, you can sail through this neighborhood by narrowboat on multiple canal waterways. Narrowboats are constructed specifically for travel on these slender canals. Each must be under **7 feet wide**, with a maximum length of **72 feet**—anything bigger just wouldn't fit!

After your canal tour, stop by the area's many cafés and restaurants for a special waterside meal. Wave to the boats as they pass by!

WHERE TO NEXT?

See a rainbow of colorful homes! Turn to page **68**.

Hail a cab, it's time to go! Turn to page **70**.

When London is dreary and gray, head to this colorful neighborhood to brighten your day!

NOTTING HILL is a popular area in West London known for its vibrant townhouses. These beautiful homes have been painted in a rainbow of colors over the years, from pastel blue to sunshine yellow—even magenta!

A two-mile stroll will lead you through Portobello Road, the world's largest antiques market, with over **1,000 dealers** selling nearly every kind of collectible you can imagine. From stamps and jewelry to furniture and vintage clothing, there's lots to discover at these quirky shops.

The sun is starting to set—let's grab a taxi, quick!

TURN THE PAGE

Black cabs can take you to any destination—
The drivers are experts on all things London!

Ask them anything! Being in a **BLACK CAB** is like having
a personal tour guide—the drivers know all about the city and are
happy to share their tips and insight on what to do and see.

Before receiving their taxi license, the drivers go through a rigorous training process to attain "the knowledge." They attend school, pass many tests, and learn **60,000 street names**—as well as every restaurant, monument, and government building of interest that a passenger might want to visit!

TURN THE PAGE

BONG! **BIG BEN** rings out on the hour all the way up in Elizabeth Tower!

The name "Big Ben" doesn't refer to the clock tower itself; it's the nickname given to the enormous **13-ton Great Bell** inside the structure. The tower's proper name is the Elizabeth Tower, and at **315 feet tall**, it is one of the most famous landmarks in Europe.

Big Ben is known for being an excellent timekeeper! Its bong marks each hour with perfect accuracy. The sound can be heard echoing for up to five miles across the city.

BONG! Big Ben rings out once again, signaling that our adventure in London has—for now—come to an end.

⇉ ADVENTURE INDEX ⇇

Want to learn even more about London? We've compiled fun facts, history, and helpful hints about favorite locations to help you explore further during your city journey!

TOWER BRIDGE Pages 2–3

See the bridge lift for a passing ship! The Tower Bridge opens between 700 to 1,000 times each year to provide access to large vessels. The entire process takes approximately 3 minutes and is fun to watch. The lift times are posted in advance to help you plan. **Tower Bridge Road, London SE1 2UP • towerbridge.org.uk/lift-times**

Nearby Adventures

THE SHARD At more than 1,000 feet tall, London's best view can be found at the Shard! The pyramid-shaped glass tower is one of the tallest buildings in Europe, allowing for a view of 40 miles across the capital. **32 London Bridge Street, London SE1 9SG • the-shard.com**

HMS BELFAST Step onboard the HMS *Belfast* to see what life was like on board a working World War II warship. **The Queens Walk, London SE1 2JH • iwm.org.uk/visits/hms-belfast**

GIRL WITH A DOLPHIN FOUNTAIN This whimsical fountain sits right on the water. The backdrop of the bridge makes it a great photo op! **Tower Bridge, London E1W 1LD • hrp.org.uk/tower-of-london**

TOWER OF LONDON Pages 4–5

After the doors close and the sun sets, a few lucky guests can attend the Tower of London's nightly Ceremony of the Keys: the historical securing of the tower gates when the Chief Yeoman Warder locks up the doors and passes on the Queens Keys for safekeeping. This popular experience books months in advance. **Tower of London EC3N 4AB • hrp.org.uk/tower-of-london/whats-on/ceremony-of-the-keys**

Nearby Adventures

SKY GARDEN Copy that! Head to the viewing gallery on the 35th floor of the "Walkie-Talkie" building for panoramic views over London. Stroll through the gardens before making your way to the observation deck and open-air terrace. The view is amazing! **1 Sky Garden Walk, London EC3M 8AF • skygarden.london**

COPPA CLUB Dine inside an igloo! Just steps from the Tower, the Coppa Club offers private dining "igloos" overlooking the Tower Bridge and Thames River. Book your reservation well in advance. **3 Quays Walk, Lower Thames Street, Tower, London EC3R 6AH • coppaclub.co.uk**

BOROUGH MARKET Pages 6–7

A feast for the eyes and the stomach, Borough Market is over 1,000 years old and London's oldest food market. Purchase fresh produce from all around Britain, including fish and seafood, cheeses, meats, fruits, and vegetables. Come hungry! **8 Southwark Street, London SE1 1 • boroughmarket.org.uk**

Nearby Adventures

LONDON BRIDGE EXPERIENCE Take a trip into the Bridge's history and spooky haunted tunnels at London's scariest theatrical experience. Not for the faint of heart! **2–4 Tooley Street, London SE1 2SY • thelondonbridgeexperience.com**

SOUTHWALK CATHEDRAL Swing by the cathedral to learn more about the famous feline Doorkins Magnificat, who called the cathedral home. **Montague Close, London SE1 9DA • cathedral. southwark.anglican.org/visiting/doorkins-magnificat**

CLINK PRISON MUSEUM Go behind the bars at England's oldest and most notorious prison. **1 Clink Street, SE1 9DG • clink.co.uk**

ST. PAUL'S CATHEDRAL Pages 8–9

An icon of London's skyline for more than 300 years, St. Paul's has often found its way into pop culture. A favorite moment for many is the use of the cathedral's steps in the set for the iconic "Feed the Birds" song from the Disney film version of *Mary Poppins*. **St. Paul's Churchyard, London EC4M 8AD • stpauls.co.uk**

Nearby Adventures

MONUMENT TO THE GREAT FIRE OF LONDON This London landmark was built to commemorate the Great Fire of 1666. Walk up the 311 steps of a narrow spiral staircase to reach the viewing platform. You will be rewarded with not just a great city view but also a keepsake certificate certifying that you completed the climb. **Monument Street, London EC3R 8AH • themonument.org.uk**

MILLENNIUM BRIDGE Check out the views from this modern pedestrian-only bridge that stretches across the Thames, linking St. Paul's Cathedral with the South Bank's Tate Modern. **Thames Embankment, London SE1 9JE**

ST. BRIDE'S CHURCH Can you count the 5 layers on the church's steeple? It's said to be the inspiration for traditional wedding cakes. **St. Bride's Church, Fleet Street, London, EC4Y 8AU • stbrides.com**

THE GLOBE THEATRE Pages 10–11

Originally built in 1599, the Globe had 3 stories of seating and was able to hold 3,000 spectators. The base of the stage held "the groundlings," an area where you could pay a penny to stand

and watch a performance. More than a penny today, these "pit" tickets are still available and are the cheapest way to catch a show. **21 New Globe Walk, Bankside, London SE1 9DT • shakespearesglobe.com**

Nearby Adventures

MONS CHEESEMONGERS Say cheese! Sample some of the best French and Swiss cheese at this popular store. **Voyager Business Park, Unit 2, London SE16 4RP • mons-cheese.co.uk**

GOLDEN HINDE Climb aboard this historic museum and tour a reconstruction of Sir Francis Drake's ship, which he sailed around the globe in the 1500s. **St. Mary Overie Dock, Cathedral Street, London SE1 9DE • goldenhinde.co.uk**

TATE MODERN Pages 12–13

The Tate Modern holds the nation's collection of modern art and takes the crown as the best art space in London. The galleries are arranged by theme and change frequently. Be sure to stop at the Tate's Bookshop! It is considered the best art bookshop in London and carries a wide selection of illustrated children's books on visual arts. **Bankside, London SE1 9TG • tate.org.uk/ visit/tate-modern**

TOP OF THE TATE After your art adventure, head up to the museum's top floor! There is an open viewing terrace where you can marvel at the view of the River Thames, St. Paul's Cathedral, and as far as Wembley Stadium. **Bankside, London SE1 9TG • tate. org.uk/visit/tate-modern**

Nearby Adventures

SHAKESPEARE'S GLOBE Right next door is this replica of the famous London playhouse where the Bard's plays were performed. (For more information, see "The Globe Theatre," above.) **21 New Globe Walk, London SE1 9DT • shakespearesglobe.com**

BANKSIDE BEACH While there is no swimming allowed, you can still put your toes in the sand and build a castle at this riverside beach. **Bankside, London SE1**

TELEPHONE BOX Page 14

5 Fun Facts about the Telephone Box

1. The boxes are actually just that: a box! Most telephone booths now sit empty and are nonfunctional artifacts. A lucky few boxes are getting a new lease on life by being recycled into small public libraries and even miniature art galleries!

2. The technical name for a telephone box is a "kiosk."

3. There have been many versions! Concrete was used to construct the earliest designs. Iron was used to manufacture the later versions.

4. Hats off to the design! Adapting to fashions of the time, the phone kiosk has a dome shape at top, designed specifically to allow room for a top hat.

5. The original boxes were designed to be green and silver, but the Post Office rejected the green, saying it would blend in with trees and be a dangerous road hazard.

PILLAR BOX & POSTAL MUSEUM Pages 14–15

5 Fun Facts about the Postal Service

1. Royal Mail's origins date back almost 500 years! King Henry VIII created the position of Master of the Posts in 1516.

2. When delivering letters became available to the public in 1635, the recipient had to cover the cost of the delivery!

3. The "Penny Black" was the first adhesive postage stamp, created in 1840.

4. London got its first pillar boxes in 1855; they were rectangular in shape and sage green in color. It was not until 1874 that they were painted the now-familiar red.

5. The Royal Mail had its own secret underground railway network in London. "Mail Rail" ran between London's sorting offices (also known as District Offices) and some railway stations from 1927 to 2003.

FISH AND CHIPS Pages 16–17

5 Favorite Fish-and-Chips Restaurants

The first London fish-and-chips shop opened in 1860. Today there are thousands of these "chippies" across the city. Here are a few popular locations:

POPPIES FISH AND CHIPS If you're searching for the best fish-and-chips, Poppies wears the crown as having the best in London. Multiple locations. Listed here is the original. **6–8 Hanbury Street, London E1 6QR** • poppiesfishandchips.co.uk

ROCK & SOLE PLAICE One of the oldest chippies in town, Rock & Sole Plaice has been serving London since 1871. **47 Endell Street, Covent Garden, London WC2H 9AJ** • rockandsoleplaice.com

MASTERS SUPERFISH An old-school chippie, Masters Superfish is a South London institution that is known for large portions. **191 Waterloo Road, London SE1 8UX** • masterssuperfish.has.restaurant

THE GOLDEN HIND Be forewarned: the Golden Hind doesn't take reservations, so be prepared to wait in line. **73 Marylebone Lane, Marylebone, London W1U 2PN** • goldenhindrestaurant.com

NORTH SEA FISH RESTAURANT A restaurant so famous that it's a landmark London cabbies are required to know when learning "The Knowledge" (see page 70). **7/8 Leigh Street, London WC1H 9EW** • northseafishrestaurant.co.uk

THAMES RIVER Pages 18–19

Over 200 miles and with 200 bridges, the River Thames cuts through the center of London and runs right next to many skyscrapers and iconic landmarks. Play a game of eye spy as you cruise by! How many of the following destinations can you spot?

- ☐ Shakespeare's Globe Theatre
- ☐ Tower Bridge
- ☐ St. Paul's Cathedral
- ☐ London Bridge
- ☐ The "Gherkin"
- ☐ Millennium Bridge
- ☐ The Shard

LONDON EYE Pages 20–21

Take flight into London's sky while riding inside the world's tallest cantilevered observation wheel! Each ride—or "flight"—takes 30 minutes and offers an epic bird's-eye views of London. **Westminster Bridge Road Riverside Building, County Hall, London SE1 7PB · londoneye.com**

Nearby Adventures

LONDON DUNGEON Enter if you dare! This haunted experience is based on real stories of London's gruesome past. **County Hall, Westminster Bridge Road London SE1 7PB · thedungeons.com/london**

SEA LIFE LONDON AQUARIUM Dive into an underwater adventure at one of the largest aquariums in Europe. **County Hall Westminster Bridge Road County Hall, London SE1 7PB · visitsealife.com/london**

GOLDEN CAROUSEL Jump into the saddle of one of the galloping horses on this carousel located just steps from the London Eye and river amusements. **South Bank, between Hungerford Bridge and the London Eye**

TRAFALGAR SQUARE & LIONS

Pages 22–23

Trafalgar Square is one of London's most visited spots and is considered the epicenter of the city. You will find four giant stone lions, fountains, and numerous statues. During your visit, be sure to not feed the pigeons—it is strictly forbidden!

Nearby Adventures

SHERLOCK HOMES PUB This restaurant has a quirky secret. Head up to the second floor to find a re-creation of Holmes and Watson's study and sitting room, with a large collection of objects and photographs related to the books. It's essentially a mini museum! **10 Northumberland Street, London WC2N 5DB · greeneking-pubs.co.uk**

LONDON'S SMALLEST POLICE STATION In the southeast corner of the square sits Brittan's smallest Police Station! Installed in an old lamppost in the 1920s to keep an eye on protesters, this tiny box can hold up to two prisoners at a time. **Trafalgar Square East**

THE NATIONAL GALLERY Home of one of the greatest collections of paintings in the world. The labyrinthine interior is so large, it has a color-coded map. **Trafalgar Square, London WC2N 5DN · nationalgallery.org.uk**

WESTMINSTER ABBEY Pages 24–25

The location of many royal weddings and coronations, Westminster Abbey is an important part of British history. Don't miss the Royal Tombs, Poets' Corner, and Cloisters. The tour has a great audio guide made just for children. **20 Dean's Yard, London SW1P 3PA · westminster-abbey.org**

Nearby Adventures

CHURCHILL WAR ROOMS Explore the secret underground war rooms and learn about London's World War II history at this fascinating museum. **King Charles Street, Clive Steps Westminster, London SW1A 2AQ · iwm.org.uk/visits/churchill-war-rooms**

VICTORIA TOWER GARDENS SOUTH Time for a break? Head over to this peaceful park with river views, a small playground, and memorial structures. Perfect for a picnic! **Millbank, London SW1P 3JA · royalparks.org.uk/parks/victoria-tower-gardens**

QUEEN ELIZABETH OLYMPIC PARK Pages 26–27

Home to the 2012 London Olympic Games, this sprawling 247-acre park now plays host to several sporting venues, fun playgrounds, and waterways. Champion the perfect visit by stopping by the following activities:

MAKE A SPLASH Take a dip at the London Aquatics Centre and imagine what swimming in the Olympics is like. The center offers lane swimming, classes, and family fun sessions. **Queen Elizabeth Olympic Park East · queenelizabetholympicpark.co.uk**

WATERWORKS FOUNTAINS Make a splash! Stand within a winding ribbon of 195 jets and navigate a labyrinth of computer-controlled walls of water. **Queen Elizabeth Olympic Park South · queenelizabetholympicpark.co.uk**

SWAN PADDLE BOATS Glide across the Olympic waters on a swan pedalo! These elegant paddle boats can be rented by the half hour. **Adjacent to the Aquatics Center, Queen Elizabeth Olympic Park East · leeandstortboats.co.uk**

FLOAT ON A BOAT Have a treat on a boat at the Milk Float, a docked barge that specializes in locally made ice cream, sorbets, and milkshakes. **Sweetwater Moorings, London E9 5EN • themilkfloat.com**

THE BRITISH LIBRARY Pages 28–29

This ginormous library is home to a (mind boggling!) 170 million items and counting! Fun fact: if you looked at five items in the library every day, it would take you 90,000 years to see the entire collection. **96 Euston Road, London NW1 2DB • bl.uk**

Nearby Adventures

WORD ON THE WATER Floating on Regent's Canal is London's most unique bookshop, Word on the Water. Selling everything from classics to contemporary literature, the 1920s Dutch barge bookstore is permanently docked on Granary Square. **Granary Square, London N1C 4AA • wordonthewater.co.uk**

POLLOCK'S TOY MUSEUM Displayed over four floors, this mom and pop museum showcases a quirky collection of dolls, toy theaters, teddy bears, and folk toys from around the world. **1 Scala Street, London W1T 2HL • pollockstoys.com**

EMERALD COURT A tight squeeze! See if you can walk through London's narrowest street. Emerald Court is only 26 inches at its widest! **Between Theobald's Road in WC1 and Rugby Street**

BRITISH MUSEUM Decipher the Rosetta Stone, visit the Parthenon sculptures, and unravel the history of mummies at the British Museum's remarkable collection that spans over two million years of history. **Great Russell Street, London, WC1B 3DG • britishmuseum.org**

LONDON TRANSPORT MUSEUM

Pages 30–31

Exploring the buses, trains, and taxis will make you hungry! Make a stop at the museum's on-site cafe that celebrates London Transport's design legacy with real tiles, seats, and signs reclaimed from the Underground trains. The theme continues to the food, with train-shaped pasta and Tube-themed cupcakes. **Covent Garden, London WC2E 7BB • ltmuseum.co.uk**

Nearby Adventures

ROYAL OPERA HOUSE Catch a stunning performance of music and dance—both the Royal Ballet and Royal Opera call this historic landmark home. **Covent Garden, London WC2E 9DD • roh.org.uk**

NEAL'S YARD One of London's most colorful little corners can be found tucked behind Covent Garden. Wander through a hidden passageway and into the small winding alley that leads to a colorful courtyard, home to a mix of lovely cafés, trinket shops, and charming restaurants. **Neal's Yard, London WC2H 9**

BENJAMIN POLLOCK'S TOYSHOP Puppet masters have flocked to this whimsical toy shop that's been selling vintage and retro toys for over 100 years. The store is known for its theatrical toy selection, such as paper theaters, marionettes, glove puppets, and toys that nurture storytelling. **44 The Market, Covent Garden, London WC2E 8RF • pollocks-coventgarden.co.uk**

CHINATOWN Pages 32–33

Chinatown is home to a bustling community of over 150 businesses. From shops selling lanterns and other traditional items to delicious restaurants, there's so much to explore in this neighborhood. A few stops for your visit:

GUANGHWA BOOKSHOP A literary hub for Chinese residents, tourists, and enthusiasts. Stop by for weekly calligraphy workshops and children's reading activities. **112 Shaftesbury Avenue, London W1D 5EJ • cypressbooks.com**

GOLDEN DRAGON A popular Cantonese and Peking restaurant, serving up some of the best dim sum in London. **28–29 Gerrard Street, London W1D 6JW • gdlondon.co.uk**

GOLDEN GATE CAKE SHOP Bakery that sells over 80 types of cakes. Their signature bake is Char Siu (Chinese BBQ Pork) Buns. Yum! **13 Macclesfield Street, London W1D 5BR • chinatown.co.uk/en/bar-cafe/golden-gate-cake-shop**

PICCADILLY CIRCUS W1

PICCADILLY CIRCUS Pages 34–35

Colorful and chaotic, Piccadilly Circus is one of London's most popular tourist destinations. Check out the gigantic video displays, neon signs, and famous billboards, and meet friends at the statue of Eros—one of the busiest meeting locations in the city.

Nearby Attractions

RAINFOREST CAFÉ Have a wild meal at this themed restaurant set within an exotic jungle that re-creates the sights and sounds of the Amazon rainforest. **20 Shaftesbury Avenue, London W1D 7EU • therainforestcafe.co.uk**

LEGO STORE Brick-building fanatics will love this London retail location, the largest Lego store in the world. Don't miss the life-size Underground station made completely of Legos! **3 Swiss Court, London W1D 6AP • lego.com/en-gb**

DISNEY STORE Let your imagination run free at this Oxford Street retail location. Inside you'll find the magic of Disney through wonderful toys, costumes, and merchandise. Don't miss Cinderella's golden carriage or the 28-foot-tall castle near the entrance. **350–352 Oxford Street, London W1C 1JH • stores.shopdisney.co.uk**

A SOCCER MATCH

Pages 36–37

Discover the home of one of England's top football (called soccer in the US) teams when you visit Emirates Stadium, home of the Arsenal. Score a Perfect experience with these tips for your visit.

BECOME A JUNIOR GUNNER The Arsenal Children's Club is called the Junior Gunners, which is for kids age 16 and under. Tickets for the Emirates Stadium Family Enclosure are only available to club members. **arsenal.com/juniorgunners**

EMIRATES STADIUM TOUR AND MUSEUM Soccer fans will love this tour that gives visitors access to extra-special areas: walk down the tunnel as a player and onto the pitch, where you can feel like you are part of game day action. **75 Drayton Park Emirates Stadium, London N5 1BU • arsenaldirect.arsenal.com/tour/home**

BUCKINGHAM PALACE Pages 38–39

Visitors can go behind the gates of Buckingham Palace during the summer, when the Queen is not in residence. All tours are led by a guide and include visits to state rooms, the grand staircase, and lots of history about the palace and the royal family. **Westminster, London SW1A 1AA • rct.uk/visit/the-state-rooms-buckingham-palace**

CHANGING OF THE GUARD This impressive ceremony takes place several times a week. It is sometimes canceled due to weather and scheduling changes, so be sure to check the website before your trip. Tip: Arrive early to get the best gate view! This popular procession attacks thousands of spectators. **Constitution Hill Buckingham Palace, London SW1A 1AA • householddivision.org.uk/changing-the-guard**

Other Royal Adventures

ROYAL MEWS Giddy up! The Royal Mews is one of the finest working stables in the world! Visit the fancy cars, exquisite carriages, and, best of all, the queen's horses, who live in the stables. **Buckingham Palace Road, London SW1W 1QH • rct.uk/visit/the-royal-mews-buckingham-palace**

ST JAMES'S PARK Fit for royalty, this is the most elegant park in London. It features a large lake that is a wildlife sanctuary for ducks, geese, swans, and pelicans. A perfect spot for a picnic. **Horse Guards Road, The Storeyard, London SW1A 2BJ • royalparks.org.uk/parks/st-jamess-park**

KENSINGTON PALACE PAVILION The best way to feel like royalty: have tea at a Royal Palace! Kensington Palace Pavilion is the only place in London where you can enjoy an elegant afternoon tea on the grounds of a royal palace. **Kensington Palace Green, London W8 4PX • kensingtonpalacepavilion.co.uk**

HAMPTON COURT PALACE

Pages 40–41

Complete the maze and head over to the Magic Garden, an enchanted playground with a large dragon, a bejeweled crown, a mythical beast's lair—all based on myths, stories, and real objects found at the palace. **Hampton Court Palace, East Molesey KT8 9AU • hrp.org.uk/hampton-court-palace**

More to Discover at the Palace

THE CLOCK COURT Check the time at the Clock Court, home to the astronomical clock made for Henry VIII in 1540. This unique timepiece is 15 feet across and has separate dials indicating the hour, month, and day of the week, high tides, the position of the sun, and signs of the Zodiac.

TENNIS COURT Sports fan? Run over to the Hampton Court Palace's tennis court—it's the oldest in the world!

THE TUDOR KITCHENS No dishwashers here! See what it was like to cook for 800 people 230 years ago at this fascinating Tudor kitchen that is over 36,000 square feet.

ROYAL OBSERVATORY Pages 42–43

It's about time to visit the Royal Observatory! Whether you're gazing at the stars, standing on the Prime Meridian, or marveling at the incredible timepieces, this spot provides a treasure trove of fascinating information on time.

Nearby Adventures

THE FAN MUSEUM Are you a fan . . . of fans? Head over to this world's first museum dedicated to hand fans. This unique and diverse collection contains over 5,000 fans from around the world, dating from the 1100s to the present day. **12 Crooms Hill, London SE10 8ER** • thefanmuseum.org.uk

CUTTY SARK Step on board the *Cutty Sark*, the world's only remaining Tea Clipper; it was built in 1869 to bring the freshest teas back to London. Stay after your visit for a unique tea experience that takes place on the ship under the shining coper-clad hull. **King William Walk Greenwich, London SE10 9HT** • rmg.co.uk/cutty-sark

DEER PARK Don't miss The Wilderness—Deer Park, the oldest of London's deer parks, which is an enclosed space for deer to run free. This park is home to a large red and fallow herd. **Charlton Way, London SE10 8QY** • royalparks.org.uk/parks/greenwich-park/things-to-see-and-do/wildlife

THE TUBE Pages 44–45

Five Fun Facts about London's Underground

1. The London Underground opened in 1863, becoming the first underground railway train on the planet.

2. The Underground is the third busiest metro system in Europe, after Moscow and Paris.

3. Over 2 million Tube journeys are made on the Underground every day!

4. Despite the name, almost 60% of the London Underground is actually above ground.

5. The Underground dives deep under the city! The deepest Tube station is nearly 200 feet below street level.

AFTERNOON TEA Pages 46–47

A yummy British staple, proper afternoon tea is a must-do in London! The options are endless, but we've rounded up the top unique tea-drinking experiences that are perfect for kids.

MAD HATTERS AFTERNOON TEA Tumble down the rabbit hole to enjoy an afternoon tea inspired by Alice in Wonderland. The tea includes themed details such as sealed bottle potions with a "Drink Me" tag and teapots featuring kings and queens. **50 Berners Street, Fitzrovia, London W1T3NG** • sbe.com

CHARLIE AND THE CHOCOLATE FACTORY TEA You don't need a golden ticket for this fun experience based on Roald Dahl's classic story. The tea here includes savories such as fizzy drinks, chocolate milkshakes, and, of course, chocolate factory tea. **1 Aldwych London WC2B 4B** • onealdwych.com

SCIENCE TEA Inspired by the neighboring Science Museum, this themed tea is a blast for those interested in science. Decorate scones with test tube toppings, snack on petri dish jams, and dig for a chocolate fossil in a box of "soil." **10 Harrington Road, London SW7 3ER** • ampersandhotel.com

B BAKERY AFTERNOON TEA BUS Tour and a Tea! This traditional tea consists of sandwiches, cakes, and scones and is served in a very unusual setting—a red double-decker bus while it drives around town! **Multiple departure points** • b-bakery.com

MARY POPPINS AFTERNOON TEA AT THE SHARD Practically perfect in every way, this tea is not only themed around the film classic, it's located on the 31st floor of the Shard, offering incredible sky-high views across London. **32 London Bridge Street, London SE1 9SG · the-shard.com**

NATURAL HISTORY MUSEUM

Pages 48–49

Take a deep dive into marine history by visiting the museum's beloved resident, Hope. The 82-foot 4.5-ton blue whale skeleton plunges down from the ceiling, magically swimming above visitors. **Cromwell Road, London SW7 5BD · nhm.ac.uk**

Nearby Adventures

VICTOR AND ALBERT MUSEUM The world's largest museum of applied and decorative arts and design, the Victoria and Albert Museum (commonly called V+A) has over 2.3 million objects to discover. **Cromwell Road, London SW7 2RL · vam.ac.uk**

SCIENCE MUSEUM Take flight to the Science Museum for its popular aviation and space exhibits and to see the world's oldest steam locomotive. **Exhibition Road, London SW7 2 · sciencemuseum.org.uk**

HARRODS A store so fancy it has a dress code to enter: no torn jeans and no backpacks allowed! Don't miss the toy section on the 4th floor during your visit. **87–135 Brompton Road, Knightsbridge, London SW1X 7XL · harrods.com**

STONEHENGE Pages 50–51

Stonehenge is believed to be over 5,000 years old! However, the questions surrounding the prehistoric structure may never be solved. Here are a few of the mysteries:

1. Work started on this circle around 5,000 years ago– but it took over 1,000 years to build in multiple stages. How many versions were there?

2. The bigger stones each weigh over 25 tons. How could people thousands of years ago move such heavy objects?

3. Some of the stones were transported more than 150 miles—that's the distance between Philadelphia and Washington, DC! Why did they use stones that were so far away?

4. Several stones line up with celestial events, such as the winter solstice. Was this on purpose, or just a coincidence?

5. Many believe that the stones have miraculous powers, curing people from illness and disease. Where these stones magic?

KINGS CROSS STATION Page 52

Harry Potter Fan? Walk in the footsteps of the boy magician and his Hogwarts friends by exploring these London locations that were used in the film series:

LEADENHALL MARKET This covered market with a painted roof was used as Diagon Alley in *Harry Potter and the Philosopher's Stone*. The entrance to wizard's pub, the Leaky Cauldron, is an optician's office in Bull's Head Passage. **Gracechurch Street, London EC3V 1LT · leadenhallmarket.co.uk**

HIGH COMISSION OF AUSTRALIA Scenes for Gringotts Wizarding Bank in *Harry Potter and the Philosopher's Stone* were filmed inside this building. **Strand, London WC2B 4LA · uk.embassy.gov.au**

MILLENNIUM FOOTBRIDGE The film *Harry Potter and the Half-Blood Prince* opens with a dramatic sequence of London's Millennium Footbridge collapsing. **Thames Embankment, London SE1 9JE**

THE LEWIS CHESSMAN PIECES The inspiration for the chess pieces that magically came to life in the film *Harry Potter and the Philosopher's Stone* can be found at the British Museum. **Great Russell Street, London WC1B 3DG · britishmuseum.org**

HARRY POTTER STUDIO TOUR Walk in Harry's footsteps and get an exciting peek into the making of the films. Located just outside London, this Warner Bros. Studio tour is a great day trip to discover a treasure trove of authentic movie sets, props, costumes, and memorabilia. **Studio Tour Drive, Watford, England WD25 7LR · wbstudiotour.co.uk**

THE DOUBLE-DECKER BUS Page 53

Hop on Board

Get an Oyster card and hop on the bus for a ride around the city, or simply tap a contactless credit card to the scanner. It's a flat fare no matter how far you travel! Now, where to go? These are our favorite routes:

BUS ROUTE 35: LONDON'S MARKETS Take this route and spend a day exploring markets across the city, which sell everything from clothing to food to flowers. Stops include Brixton Market, Borough Market, Brick Lane Market, Leadenhall Market, and Columbia Road Flower Market.

BUS ROUTE 139: CLASSIC LONDON Take this route and see the capital's most iconic attractions, including the Abbey Road Crossing, Piccadilly Circus and Trafalgar Square, and famous shops such as Hamleys Toy Store and Selfridges. Don't miss the view from the Waterloo Bridge!

BUS ROUTE 9: LONDON'S MUSEUMS AND PALACES Take this route to explore several royal residences, including St James's Palace and Kensington Palace, as well as the London Transport and Natural History Museum. The route includes other iconic London locations, such as Trafalgar Square.

ZSL LONDON ZOO Pages 54–55

One of the world's most famous children's characters came from the London Zoo! A black bear named Winnie lived there in the early 1900s. A visit to the zoo inspired author Alan Alexander Milne to write the Winne the Pooh stories after seeing Winnie with his son, Christopher Robin. **Regent's Park, London NW1 4RY** · zsl.org/london

Nearby Adventures

SHERLOCK HOMES MUSEUM Are you a supersleuth? Unlock the mysteries of Sherlock Holmes's cases at this museum dedicated to the world's most famous detective. **221B Baker Street, London NW1 6XE** · sherlock-holmes.co.uk

PRIMROSE HILL Paddington Bear fans will recognize colorful Chalcot Crescent, located just off Primrose Hill, Paddington's "home" featured in the films. Be sure to climb to the top of Primrose Hill, which offers one of the best free views in London. **Primrose Hill Road, London NW3**

ABBEY ROAD The most famous crosswalk in the world is a must-see stop for Beatles fans! Grab three friends and stroll across the zebra-stripe-painted intersection, capturing the iconic cover from the group's classic 1969 album. **3 Abbey Road, London NW8 9AY**

HYDE PARK Pages 56–57

Covering 350 acres encompassing a large lake, lush meadow, and flower gardens, it's easy to declare Hyde Park the best in London. Be sure not to miss these amazing activities during your visit:

BOAT ON THE SERPENTINE Pedal yourself or hire pedalos and explore Hyde Park's Serpentine River. Boat rentals are available by the half hour. **Serpentine Road, Hyde Park, London W2 2UH** · **solarshuttle.co.uk**

PRINCESS DIANA MEMORIAL PLAYGROUND Said to be one of the best playgrounds in the world, the Diana Memorial Playground attracts nearly one million visitors a year. Peter Pan themed with a large pirate ship centerpiece, the playground features a sensory trail, play sculptures, and onsite cafe. **Kensington Gardens, Broad Walk, London W2 4RU** · royalparks.org.uk/parks/kensington-gardens

PETER PAN STATUE Celebrating Kensington Garden's famous fictional resident, the bronze statue features the eternal boy surrounded by squirrels, rabbits, mice, and fairy friends. **Kensington Gardens, London W11 1PN**

THE WEST END (THEATERLAND)
Pages 58–59

Most of the city's theaters are located in the West End, which contains nearly 40 theaters offering a wide variety of shows, plays, and musicals for all ages. Family favorites include *The Wizard of Oz*, *The Lion King*, *Harry Potter*, and *Mary Poppins*.

TICKET TIME For last-minute and discounted theater tickets, head to the TKTS ticket booth in the heart of Leicester Square. The discounted tickets are available in person only for performances on that day, the next day, or up to a week in advance. **The Lodge, Leicester Square, London WC2H 7D** · officiallondontheatre.com/tkts

Pre- or Post-Theater Dinner

TREDWELLS Bring budding gourmets here to try the "Culinary Kids" menu. Offering six courses, it seeks to introduce new flavors and textures to young palates. **4A Upper St Martin's Lane, London WC2H 9NY · tredwells.com**

INAMO Dinner is a game (and keeps everyone entertained!) with the fun, interactive tables at Inamo, where visitors can play games and even watch the chefs preparing their pan-Asian fare. **134–136 Wardour Street, London W1F 8ZP · inamo-restaurant.com**

HAMLEYS TOY SHOP Pages 60–61

Hamleys has sold millions of bears! So many that if you lined them up from head to paw, the bears would stretch all the way from London to New York City. **188–196 Regent Street, London W1B 5BT · hamleys.com**

CARTOON MUSEUM Dedicated to British cartoons, caricatures, comic strips, and animation, the Cartoon Museum allows you to dip into a dazzling collection of more than 8,000 books and comics. **63 Wells Street, London W1A 3AE · cartoonmuseum.org**

SKETCH LONDON Pretty in pink! This Instagram-famous restaurant is known for the different rooms that host a variety of themes, such as the Gallery, where everything is pink. Don't miss the loos! Each bathroom is a space-age "pod" cubicle, with a ceiling of rainbow-colored tiles. **9 Conduit Street, London W1S 2XG · sketch.london**

DAUNT BOOKS Wander inside Daunt Books and you're sure to find plenty of travel books to help on your next adventure. This shop famously specializes in travel books and literature. **83–84 Marylebone High Street, London W1U 4QW · dauntbooks.co.uk**

DOUBLE-DECKER BUS RIDE

Pages 62–63

5 Fun Facts about the Double-Decker Bus

1. Originally established in London in 1829, the first buses could carry a group of people and were pulled by three horses!

2. The first London Bus fare cost only one shilling!

3. The first bus service was called Omnibus, which means "for all" in Latin.

4. Buses on country routes have been known to be painted green to better fit in with their natural surroundings.

5. During the week, London buses carry up to 6 million passengers per day.

BRICK LANE Pages 64–65

This neighborhood is the heart of the Bangladeshi community in the United Kingdom. You'll find incredible vintage clothing and bric-a-brac markets, top graffiti stops, and the best curry in the city! Here are a few stops for your visit:

CITY SPICE Located at the heart of Brick Lane, this curry house offers a mix of Bengali, Mughal, and classic Indian cuisines. It's a popular spot for celebrities, too. **138 Brick Lane, London E1 6RU · city-spice.london**

BEIGEL BAKE This Brick Lane bakery is the oldest and best bagel shop in London. A bustling 24-hour-a-day restaurant, Beigel Bake makes over 7,000 bagels a night. Popular favorites include hot salt beef and salmon with cream cheese. **159 Brick Lane, London E1 6SB · bricklanebeigel.co.uk**

STREET ART Brick Lane is like a street gallery, with amazing art to be found throughout the neighborhood. The works change constantly, sometimes on a weekly basis. Look in these spots during your visit for some of the larger concentrations: **Seven Stars Yard, Buxton Street, Princelet Street**, and **Hanbury Street.**

BRICK LANE MARKET Hunt for a bargain within Brick Lane's markets, full of food stalls, antiques, fabrics, and collectibles. Weekends are the busiest and have the most vendors, where you will find indoor and outdoor markets spilling into each other. One of the largest: **Upmarket, Ely's Yard, E1 6QR · sundayupmarket.co.uk**

LITTLE VENICE Pages 66–67

Brimming with colorful houseboats and cute cafés, Little Venice is a fun way to spend the day. Glide down the canals by narrowboat, or stroll the pretty streets by foot. A few fun stops:

PUPPET THEATER BARGE Dance on over to this unique fifty-seat marionette theater on a converted barge. It is docked in Little Venice throughout the year. **Blomfield Road, Little Venice, London W9 2PF · puppetbarge.com**

LONDON WATERBUS All aboard! Take to the water for a narrowboat ride through Little Venice. Be sure to grab a window seat—the route travels directly through the London Zoo. **Located below Blomfield Road on the canal towpath · londonwaterbus.com**

WATERSIDE CAFÉ Have lunch while you float on a narrowboat at this restaurant located on a boat docked on the Grand Union Canal. **Warwick Crescent Little Venice, W2 6NE · waterside-cafe.co.uk**

NOTTING HILL Pages 68–69

Stroll the quaint streets of colorful townhouses and visit the famous Portobello Market. Visit in August during the Bank Holiday to see the area come alive with Europe's biggest street festival, the Notting Hill Carnival. **nhcarnival.org**

SPOT PRETTY PASTEL HOUSES Notting Hill is home to several quiet streets with pretty pastel houses that have multicolor terraces. Be sure not to miss **Lancaster Road**, **Elgin Crescent**, **Hillgate Street,** and **Portobello Road**.

DECORATE BISCUITS AT BISCUITEERS The famous black-and-white facade is enough reason for a stop at this yummy bakery! Come hungry for biscuits and cupcakes adorned with Biscuiteers famous icing and try your own hand at decorating at the popular Icing School. **194 Kensington Park Road London, W11 2ES · biscuiteers.com**

THE CHURCHILL ARMS Stop to smell the flowers! The Churchill Arms has an impressive (and super famous!) flower display that covers the exterior. It's rumored they spend up to £25,000 ($33,000) a year on their unique floral displays! **119 Kensington Church Street, London W8 7LN · churchillarmskensington.co.uk**

BLACK CAB Pages 70–71

5 Fun Facts about London's Black Cabs

1. Taxis are available if the light at the top is lit. If it's off, they are off duty or already carrying passengers.

2. No need to shout! It's against the law to yell "Taxi!" to get a cab's attention; just hold out your arm to signal them.

3. The black cab was originally designed to have a turning circle of 25 feet. It's believed this radius was to accommodate the small roundabout at the entrance of the popular Savoy Hotel.

4. Black cabs were originally designed to be tall enough to accommodate a passenger wearing a bowler hat in the 1920s.

5. It usually takes a driver between 2 to 4 years to pass London's Black Cab drivers test.

BIG BEN Pages 72–73

Big Ben is BIG! Each dial is 23 feet in diameter, and the minute hands are 14 feet long. Although the tower is not open to the public, U.K. residents can arrange a visit by writing to their member of Parliament. **Houses of Parliament, Westminster, London · parliament.uk**

HOUSES OF PARLIAMENT The Palace of Westminster is where Britain's members of Parliament meet. The building has 100 stairwells, 11 courtyards, 1,100 offices, 3 miles of corridor, and its own gymnasium, shooting range, and hair salon! **Parliament Square, London SW1A 0AA · parliament.uk**

Nearby Adventures

WESTMINSTER BRIDGE Constructed in 1862, this is one of the oldest bridges in London. Its green color matches the leather seats in the House of Commons.

CITY CRUISES Just steps from Big Ben is the Westminster Millennium Pier, home to the City Cruises Terminal. Hop onboard for breathtaking views from the open upper deck on a River Thames sightseeing cruise. **Westminster Pier, Victoria Embankment, London SW1A 2JH · citycruises.com**